THE SECRET LIVES
OF TEACHERS

CHOSEN BY
BRIAN MOSES

ILLUSTRATED BY
LUCY MADDISON

MACMILLAN CHILDREN'S BOOKS

First published 1996 by
Macmillan Children's Books
a division of Macmillan Publishers Ltd
25 Eccleston Place London SW1W 9NF
and Basingstoke

Associated companies throughout the world

ISBN 0 330 342657

19 18 17 16 15 14 13 12 11 10

A CIP catalogue record for this book is available from the British
Library.

Printed in Great Britain

Where Do All The Teachers Go? by Peter Dixon © 1988 was first published in Grow
Your Own Poems by Macmillan Education.
Bogeyman Headmaster by John Agard © 1990 was first published in Laughter Is An
Egg by the Penguin Group.

CONTENTS

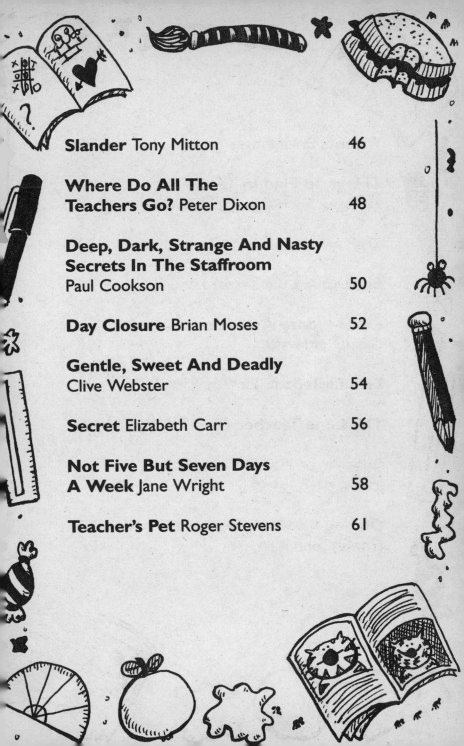

What Teachers Wear In Bed!

It's anybody's guess
what teachers wear in bed at night
so we held a competition
to see if any of us were right.

We did a spot of research,
although some of them wouldn't say,
but it's probably something funny
as they look pretty strange by day.

Our Headteacher's quite old-fashioned,
he wears a Victorian nightshirt,
our sports teacher wears her tracksuit
and sometimes her netball skirt.

That new teacher in the infants
wears bedsocks with see-through pyjamas,
our Deputy Head wears a T-shirt
he brought back from the Bahamas.

We asked our secretary what she wore
but she shooed us out of her room,
and our teacher said, her favourite nightie
and a splash of expensive perfume.

And Mademoiselle, who teaches French,
is really very rude,
she whispered, '*Alors*! Don't tell a soul,
but I sleep in the . . . back bedroom!'

Brian Moses

Ms Spry

Sweet Miss Spry
Seems rather shy,
But Ben and I
Think she's a spy,
Living in a shady dive
And being paid by MI5.

John Kitching

Do You Know My Teacher?

(female teacher version)

(fill in the word you think is most appropriate)

She's got a piercing stare and long black . . .
a) teeth
b) shoes
c) moustache
d) hair

She eats chips and beef and has short sharp . . .
a) doorstoppers
b) fangs
c) nails
d) teef

She is slinky and thin and has a pointed . . .
a) banana
b) chin
c) beard
d) umbrella

She has a long straight r and hairy little . . .
a) kneecaps
b) ears
c) children
d) toes

She has sparkling eyes
and wears school . . .
a) dinners
b) trousers
c) ties
d) buses

She comes from down
south and has a very big . . .
a) handbag
b) vocabulary
c) mouth
d) eggcup

She yells like a preacher
yes, that's my . . .
a) budgie
b) stick
c) padlock
d) teecha!

John Rice

15

16

Miss Mooney

Miss Mooney's gone all moony,
not with-it anymore,
staring out the window,
looking at the floor.

Miss Mooney's gone all mopey,
there's a funny look in her eyes,
gazing up at the ceiling,
breathing hefty sighs.

We have a theory:
ever since he came,
that new Mr Pritchard,
she's not been the same!

Mind you, he is dishy,
and Class Three says he's fun . . .
lucky old Class Three then!
unlucky us Class One!

Miss Mooney's gone all gawpy,
in Poetry today
she read 'My Love Is Like a Red Red Rose':
what more is there to say!

Matt Simpson

Head Teacher Flips Her Lid

Look – there's the Head Teacher!
The one over there!
She's stormed from her office,
she's torn out her hair,
she's punching the door,
she's kicking the wall,
she's doing a head stand
on top of a stool,
she's doing a cart-wheel
in front of the class,
her eyes are all bloodshot,
her mouth's full of grass,
she's flinging her arms up,
she's beating her breast,
she's spray-canned the playground

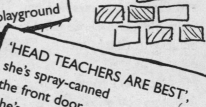

head
teacher
woz
ere

'HEAD TEACHERS ARE BEST',
she's spray-canned
the front door,
she's spray-canned the wall
'HEAD TEACHER WOZ 'ERE'
and 'HEAD TEACHER IS COOL',
'HEAD TEACHER'S THE BRAINIEST
UNDER THE SUN',
'HEAD TEACHER IS GREAT –
SHE'S ACE, NUMBER ONE'.

She suddenly turns;
for what can she hear?
A very loud ringing
that's next to her ear.
She jumps when she sees
that she isn't alone:
her secretary's saying
'Oh, Head, it's the phone.'
She opens her eyes
with a throat-clearing cough:
'I think I was dreaming.

I must have dozed off.'

Charles Thomson

head teachers are best

head teacher rules O.K.

Through The Staffroom Door

Ten tired teachers slumped in the staffroom at playtime,
one collapsed when the coffee ran out, then there were nine.

Nine tired teachers making lists of things they hate,
one remembered playground duty, then there were eight.

Eight tired teachers thinking of holidays in Devon,
one slipped off to pack his case, then there were seven.

Seven tired teachers, weary of children's tricks,
one hid in the stock cupboard, then there were six.

Six tired teachers, under the weather, barely alive,
one gave an enormous sneeze, then there were five.

Five tired teachers, gazing at the open door,
one made a quick getaway, then there were four.

Four tired teachers, faces lined with misery,
one locked herself in the ladies, then there were three.

Three tired teachers, wondering what to do,
one started screaming when the bell rang, then there were two.

Two tired teachers, thinking life really ought to be fun,
one was summoned to see the Head, then there was one.

One tired teacher caught napping in the afternoon sun,
fled quickly from the staffroom, then there were none.

Brian Moses

Ms Sayer

Ms Sayer is lazy.
She hates waking up.
She loathes each new term.
She loves breaking up.

John Kitching

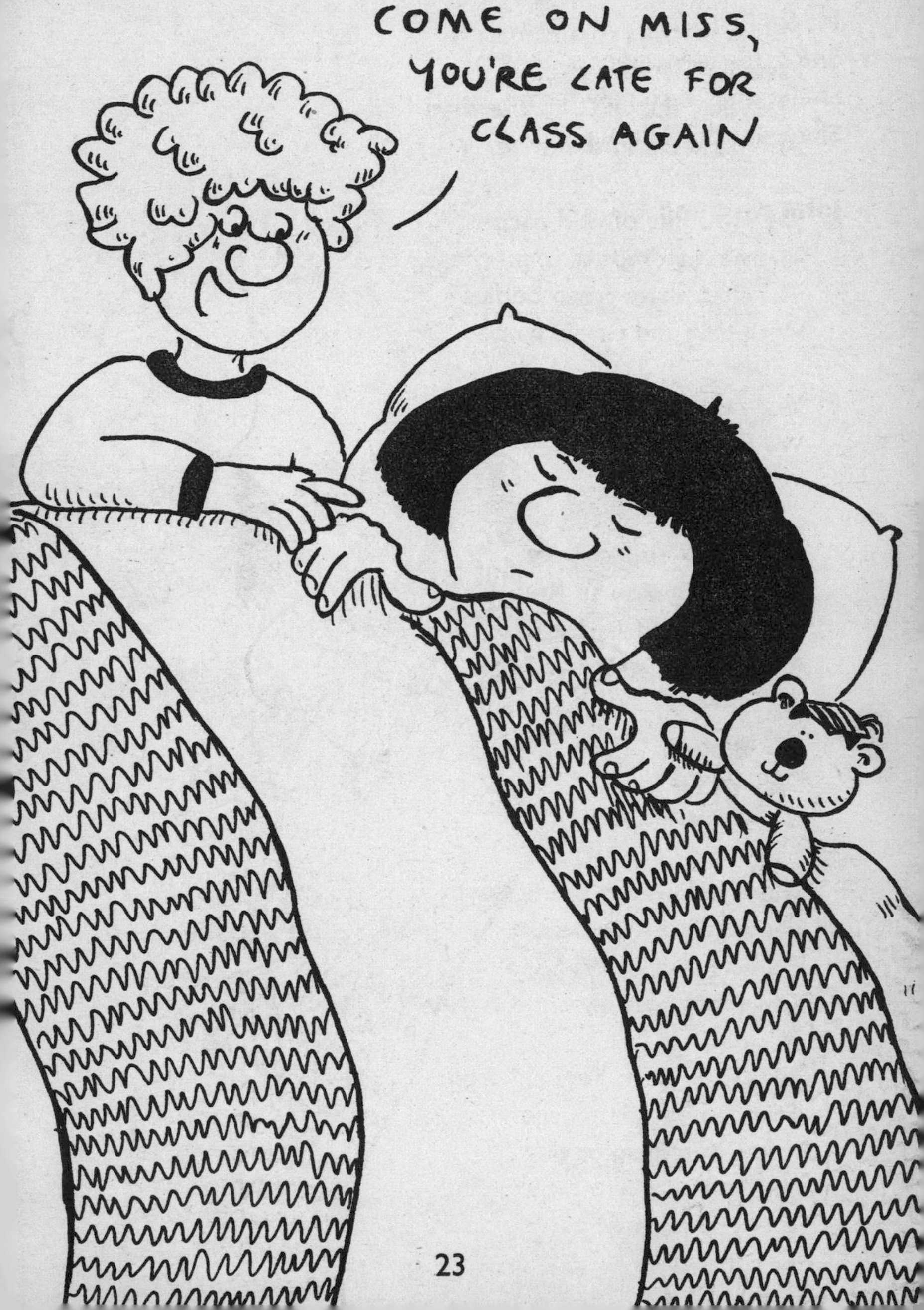
COME ON MISS, YOU'RE LATE FOR CLASS AGAIN

I Deliver Their Papers – So I Know

Miss is married to a Martian
I saw its friends arrive,
They flew the UFO up the road
And parked it in the drive.

She gives lots of wild parties;
There's hundreds of them there.
The aliens have green bodies
With pink and purple hair.

Yes, yes, it's true.
We know
We've seen it too.

Sir has got a special pet;
It's a Tyrannosaurus Rex.
He feeds it on asparagus
And abandoned ostrich eggs.

Yes, yes, it's true.
We know
We've seen it too.

The Head lives in a bungalow,
The garden's very neat,
His wife always says hello
And sometimes gives me sweets.

They've got two little children,
A cat, a dog, some mice.
I often see them playing;
They're really very nice.

You never saw that
With your own two eyes!
I don't believe it,
You're telling lies!

Trevor Millum

Our Dad Is A Teacher

Our dad is a teacher.
And if that's not bad enough,
he teaches in our school,
so we see both sides of him.

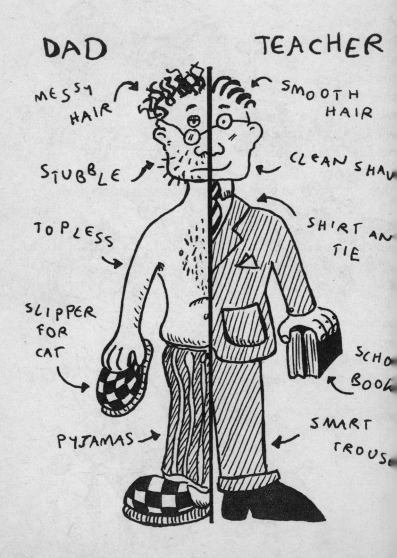

At school,
dad struts about importantly:
'don't run down the corridor'
'tuck your shirt in boy'
'get your hands out of your pockets'
'don't you DARE let me hear that word again!'

At home,
he slobs around in the morning,
showing a load of bum cleavage
because the elastic in his pyjamas is going;
then suddenly,
he streaks topless through the kitchen
with a slipper in one hand
holding up his pyjamas with the other,
screaming
that blanking cat is blanking on my blanking garden again'.

At school,
our dad is respected.
What would the kids think
if they saw him
sitting on the toilet
bathroom door open
pyjama trousers round his ankles
reading Michael Rosen poems
and singing like a Goon?

Wonder what it's worth to keep quiet?

Mike Jubb

I'M OFF!

Truants

Mr Flint drove to school each day
with Mrs Brice,
along the way they shared conversation,
shared their troubles, shared petrol money,
and then one day,
one warm bright day at the start of summer,
when the last thing they felt like doing
was teaching troublesome children,
they drove on,
right past the school gates.
Several children saw them,
several children waved
but they took no notice.
They drove on through towns and villages,
past cows and horses at rest on hillsides,
past a windmill, its sails turning lazily
until finally they could travel no more
and ahead of them stretched the sea.
Then they turned and looked at each other
and wondered what they'd done,
but as they'd driven such a long way,
they thought they might as well enjoy themselves.
So they paddled in the sea,
they skipped and chased along the beach,
they flipped stones into the water,
they built a magnificent sandcastle.
For lunch they ate ice cream and candyfloss.
Then they rode a miniature train
to the end of the pier and back,
played a double round of crazy golf,
lost lots of money in amusement arcades
and shared two bags of fish and chips
with a gang of gulls on the prom.

They drove home in silence,
past the horses and cows
and the windmill now still
past the school gates
now firmly locked for the night.

And when they sneaked back to school next day
all sheepish and shy,
embarrassed at the fuss they'd caused,
their headteacher
made them go outside at playtime
for a whole week!

Brian Moses

Things To Find In Teacher's Trouser Turn-ups

Just find any male member of staff
who wears trousers that have turn-ups
and you will usually find
that they have been wearing exactly the same pair
for years.
And years. And years.

Imagine what can be found in those turn-ups . . .
Crumbs from ancient sandwiches
Congealed curry stains
Fluff
A dead woodlouse
Flakes of chocolate
Cigarette ash
A paper clip
Bogies
Earwax that looks like yellow cheese
Yellow cheese that looks like earwax
More fluff.

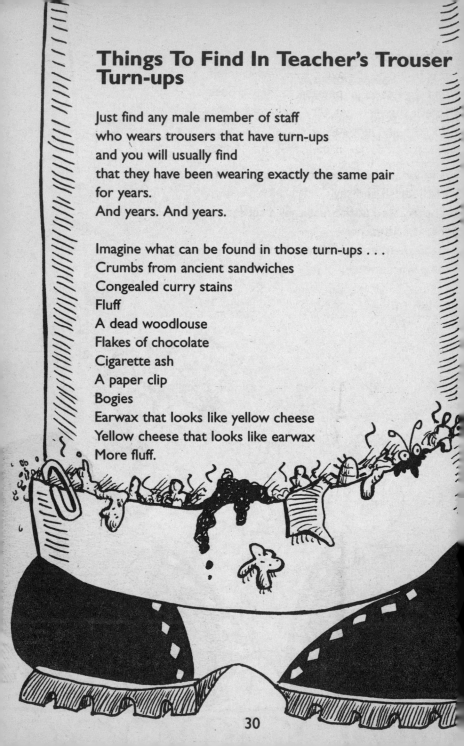

Whatever you do,
if you decide to have a look for yourself
and they see you peering at their trousers
they'll suddenly get very embarrassed
go very red indeed
and check to see if their flies are undone.

Paul Cookson

Tea

The teacher by the window
is thinking about class 4b,
the one reading the paper
is wishing she was rich,
the one chomping chocolate biscu
is dreaming of his girlfriend,
the one slurping low-fat yoghurt
is hoping her car's been fixed.

The teacher beside the door
is hoping the knocking will stop,
the student in the corner
is wondering where to sit,
the teacher by the kettle
is wishing it would boil,
the one staring wearily at the wall
is thinking her head will split.

The teacher reading the notices
is not really thinking at all,
the one with her head in a magazine
is dreaming of sun and sea,
the one in the tie is rubbing his eyes
and hoping he's not going bald,
but the teacher by the window
is thinking about class 4b,

he's the one
who just spilt his tea.

Dave Calder

Be-Bop-A-Lula

Four of our teachers have formed
A POP GROUP!

Mr Holland is on keyboards
Miss Costello sings
Mr Clapton plays guitar
Mrs Collins bashes drums.

My dad says he saw them, once,
performing in a pub.
His opinion: Well, for a bunch of teachers,
they were really rather good.

Perhaps they'll make a record.
Have a hit
and then quit school?

Tour the world as superstars?
Become hip?
And rich? And cool!

Until then
they'll have to teach us
how to read and how to write.

Hang on
to their day jobs.
Perform their music late at night

And during breaks
(if they're not
on playground duty).

Be-Bop-A-Lula a r
classic which provid-
legendary rock 'n' rolle
Gene Vincent with his
million-seller in 1956

Note: They still need a bass player.
Any volunteers?

('Be-Bop-A-Lula': a rock classic which provided legendary rock'n'roller Gene Vincent with his first million-seller in 1956.)

Bernard Young

Extra-Money Activities (night-club)

Mr Count who teaches Maths,
became a comic just for laughs.

Behind the bar is Madame Drench
who by the day takes us for French.

Dinner lady, Mrs Kipper,
took the job as part-time stripper.

Mr Smart from Art and Craft
earns more for brushing floors. It's daft!

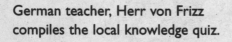

Miss Plummy-Tongue, of gentle breed,
who listens to us when we read,
at night is now attending to
the cloakroom and the ladies' loo.

German teacher, Herr von Frizz
compiles the local knowledge quiz.

Jack O'Toole, O'school caretaker,
got appointed as head waiter.

Mrs Note, the Music tutor's
ringing bells for 'TIME', in future.

(We hesitate . . . er . . . to announce . . . er . . .
the Head's applied to be a bouncer.)

Gina Douthwaite

School Report

Becky Sams
  told
    Jane Parkes
     who told
      Bee Moran
       who told Gail Pendry
      who told
        her cousin Karen
       who told
        Beth Lord
        who told
         Marilyn Cutts
        who told
         Maggie Dobbs
         who told
          Tracey Vine
         who told
          Val Clark
          who told

               me

that she'd seen
Mr Pritchard & Miss Gibbs
holding hands
& choosing satsumas
together
in Sainsbury's
on Saturday.

I told you
there was something going on
between those two –
didn't I!

Tony Langham

The Lone Teacher

We've got a new teacher
he wears a mask
and a big wide hat.

He comes to school
on a silver horse
and rides around the field
all day.

Sometimes he says
'Have you seen Toronto?'

We tell him
we haven't been to Canada
but is it near
the Panama Canal
because we did that in geography
last term.

At four o'clock
he rides off into the sunset
and comes back the next morning
in a cloud of dust.

We wonder if
he will ever come and teach us Maths
like he said he would
when he first arrived.

Perhaps then he'll tell us his name
not keep it a secret
because my dad always asks me
'Who is that man?'

David Harmer

Bogeyman Headmaster

Our headmaster is a bogeyman
Our headmaster is a bogeyman
and he'll catch you if he can.

He creeps through the window
when the school is closed at night
just to give the caretaker a fright.

Our headmaster is a bogeyman
Our headmaster is a bogeyman
and he'll catch you if he can.

When he walks
his feet never touch the ground.
When he talks
his mouth never makes a sound.
That's why assembly is so much fun.

You should see him float through the air
when we say our morning prayer
and at assembly the teachers get trembly
when the piano starts to play on its own.
It's our bogeyman headmaster having a bogeyman joke.

Only the lollipop lady doesn't feel scared
'cause when he tried his bogeyman trick
she said, 'Buzz off or I'll hit you with my stick.'

Life can be lonely
for our bogeyman headmaster
but from his office you can always hear
this strange sound of laughter.

John Agard

43

Do You Know My Teacher?

(male teacher version)

(fill in the word you think is most appropriate)

He adores pork pies
and has big blue . . .
a) legs
b) pencils
c) eyes
d) ears

MY VERY
OWN PENCIL

YOU'RE NOT VERY
TALL ARE YOU
SIR?

He's not very tall
in fact he's rather . . .
a) daft
b) old
c) bookish
d) small

HOW V
INFORM

CORN
FLAKES

He won't stand for any capers
every day he reads the . . .
a) Beano
b) dictionary
c) papers
d) Corn Flakes packet

John Rice

Slander

We all talk about the teachers
and joke about the clothes they wear.
We all talk about the ones we like
and the ones that just aren't fair.

We all talk about the teachers,
the ones that scream and yell,
the ones that keep us in at break
and even some that smell!

We all talk about the teachers
and the stupid things they say,
the things that drive us bonkers
till we feel like running away.

But yesterday I crept to the staffroom
because I'd missed my bus.
And just you wait till I tell you
the things they were saying about us!

Tony Mitton

Where Do All The Teachers Go?

Where do all the teachers go
When it's 4 o'clock?
Do they live in houses
And do they wash their socks?

Do they wear pyjamas
And do they watch TV?
And do they pick their noses
The same as you and me?

Do they live with other people
Have they mums and dads?
And were they ever children
And were they ever bad?

Did they ever, never spell right
Did they ever makes mistakes?
Were they punished in the corner
If they pinched the chocolate flakes?

Did they ever lose their hymn books
Did they ever leave their greens?
Did they scribble on the desk tops
Did they wear old dirty jeans?

I'll follow one back home today
I'll find out what they do?
Then I'll put it in a poem
That they can read to you.

Peter Dixon

Deep, Dark, Strange And Nasty Secret In The Staffroom

There are deep, dark, strange and nasty
secrets in the staffroom
when the teachers escape at break
from the confines of the classroom.
What's behind, what do we find
behind the staffroom door?
What lurks inside, what secrets hide
behind the staffroom door?

There are a thousand cups unfinished
all covered in green mould.
Coffee stains and rings remain
where they have overflowed.
Piles of files and unmarked books
and last term's lost reports,
the P.E. teacher's sweaty vest
and Lycra cycling shorts.

There are last week's lunch left-overs,
yoghurt pots and crusts,
banana skins and cola tins
all covered in chalk dust.
Examination papers
from nineteen sixty-eight
and the *Times Ed* job section
that's ten years out of date.

The ashtray's overflowed
and it's seeping out the door.
The wind has blown a million sheets
of paper on the floor.

There's paper planes and brown tea stains
from last night's staff meeting.
This place is a downright disgrace
not fit for a pig to eat in.

Inside the fridge half-finished milk
is lumpy and it's glowing.
The cartons are all starting
to mutate and they are growing.
The crockery mountain in the sink
is coated in green lime
and the room that time forgot
is left to rot in gunge and slime.

Beware the beings from this place,
the ones who always say
'No-one leaves this room
until this mess is cleared away!'
But if you said the same to them
one thing is very clear
to get the staffroom spick and span
would take them all a year
. . . or two . . . or three . . . or four

There are deep, dark, strange and nasty . . . etc.

Paul Cookson

Day Closure

We had a day closure on Monday
and I spent the morning in bed,
but the teachers went in as usual
and someone taught them instead.

And I thought of them all in the classroom,
stuck to their seats in rows,
some of them sucking pen lids,
Head Teacher scratching his nose.

Perhaps it's a bit like an MOT
to check if teachers still know
the dates of our kings and queens
or the capital of so and so.

Perhaps they had tables and spellings,
did the Head give them marks out of ten?
And then, if they got any wrong,
did he make them learn them again?

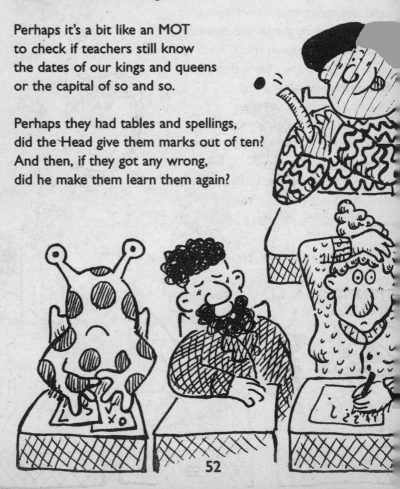

I thought of them out at break time
playing football or kiss chase or tag,
picking up teams in the playground
or scoffing crisps from a bag.

If I'd been a fly on the wall,
I might have watched while they slaved.
I'd have seen who asked silly questions
or if anyone misbehaved.

I thought of them all going home,
crossing the road to their mums.
They looked very grim the next day.
It couldn't have been much fun.

Brian Moses

Gentle, Sweet And Deadly

We always thought that our RE teacher
Was a kind and gentle lady –
Her voice was soft, and her eyes were kind.
Yes, a sweet little thing was Miss Brady.

But on Saturday, boy, did we get a shock,
We couldn't believe it was true –
Little Miss Brady had a weekend job
as a wrestler called 'Slippery Sue'!

PUT M
DOWN

A female wrestler! Little Miss Brady,
Who teaches forgiveness and peace –
Dressed in a leotard, yellow and blue,
And covered all over in grease.

She's half the size of all the others,
But because she's greasy and small
She always slips out of all of their holds,
They can't pin her down in a fall.

We saw her there, as real as can be,
On 'Saturday Sport' on the telly,
Grabbing opponents by hair and by throat,
And butting 'em all in the belly.

The crowd went wild, they chanted her name –
'Slippery, Slippery Sue.'
And there was Miss Brady, larger than life
In the ring, on the telly – it's true!
We still can't believe it's little Miss Brady –
To think how she's fooled folk for years.
Instead of just orange juice, coffee or tea
She prob'ly downs twenty-odd beers!

But now that we know, there's one thing for sure –
If we get told off by Miss Brady,
You can bet your life there'll be no back-chat –
You just can't mess with that lady.

Clive Webster

Secret

'Hey, Katie, I have something to tell you!'

'What's that?'

'I found out when I got pulled up for talking.'

'Go on then.'

'You know that Sir put me outside the classroom.'

'So what?'

'Well, that was when I saw them! They were walking . . .'

'Saw who?'

'Along the corridor outside the Maths room.'

'Oh, yeah?'

'You should have seen my face! I just sat gawping!'

'At what?'

'They never saw me, though. I kept my head down.'

'Well, tell me!'

'They held hands and her head was on his shoulder!'

'What next?'

They stopped outside the Maths room door and turned round.'

'Yes, but who?'

'Face to face, and gazing at each other.'

'Tell me, do!'

'He kissed her and she had her arms around . . .'

'For Heaven's sake!'

'His neck! I'll have to run or I'm in bother.'

'Wait, not yet!'

'I'll tell you, but promise it's a secret – '

'Yes, yes!'

'Crikey! There's the bell – I'll have to hurry'.

'I promise!'

'Don't tell anybody else I leaked it!'

'I can't hear you!'

'Miss Lavine's in love with Mr Murray.'

'SPEAK UP!'

'MISS LAVINE'S IN LOVE WITH MR MURRAY!'

Elizabeth Carr

Not Five But Seven Days A Week

Next weekend go into town
And spot the teachers all around,
They're out there practising what they preach
Not five but *seven* days a week.

They just don't get it, that they're free
For two whole days, just as they please,
Instead they're marching up and down,
Still on duty, armed with frown.

On passers-by they like to pounce –
'How many grammes are in an ounce?'
'How many Ss in Mississippi?'
'Mind your language – don't get lippy!'

PICK THAT UP NOW!

Tired shoppers can't believe the fuss –
'There'll be no talking on this bus!'
'No pushing in the check-out queue
And hands up if you want the loo.'

'No running in supermarket aisles,
Get shopping stacked in tidy piles,
No eating sweets or chewing gum,
And don't be cheeky to your mum.'

Still later when the streets have emptied,
And to their homes they can't be tempted,
You see these teachers – completely bats –
Talking multiplication with alley cats.

Jane Wright

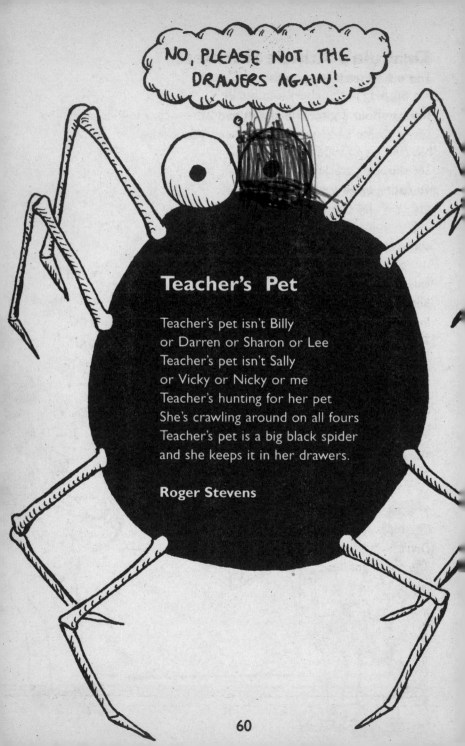

Teacher's Pet

Teacher's pet isn't Billy
or Darren or Sharon or Lee
Teacher's pet isn't Sally
or Vicky or Nicky or me
Teacher's hunting for her pet
She's crawling around on all fours
Teacher's pet is a big black spider
and she keeps it in her drawers.

Roger Stevens

Dracula's Auntie Ruthless

and other petrifying poems

Poems about ghosts and ghouls and other scary folk compiled by
David Orme and illustrated by David Woodward.

You've heard of old Drac
He's the one with the teeth
And a crumbly castle
With a tomb underneath.

Now he's bad enough
But you really just can't
Imagine the horror
That is Dracula's Aunt . . .

You can?

Well, can you imagine the rest of the gang?
There are snapping sharks, slithering snakes,
squealing skeletons and, best of all, a bathroom
gone beserk, where –

The toilet seat has teeth! Ow!
The toilet seat has teeth! Ow!
Don't – sit – on – it!
The toilet seat has . . .! Owwwww!

'Ere We Go!

Football poems compiled by David Orme, with football facts by Ian Blackman, and illustrations by Marc Vyvyan-Jones.

Football Mad

Gizza go of yer footie,
Just one belt of the ball?
Lend yer me scarf on Satdee
for just one boot at the wall?

Give yer a poster of Gazza
for one tiny kick with me right?
Do y'after be that mingey?
Go on, don't be tight!

A chest-it-down to me left foot,
a touch, a header, a dribble?
A shot between the goalie's legs,
a pass right down the middle?

Y'can borree me Madonna records
for as long as ever y'like,
I'll give yer a go around the block
on me brand new mountain bike.

One day I'll be playin' for Liverpule
wen yooze are all forgot:
go on, a titchy kick of yer footie,
one meezly penulty shot?

I'll get yer a season ticket
when I am in THE TEAM,
and wen I'm scorin' in the Cup
you'll be sittin' by the Queen.

Matt Simpson

Snoggers

Slap'n'tickle poems chosen by David Orme

A great collection of poems
for Snoggers, Sniggerers,
Slappers and Ticklers.

Snogging

They were snogging in the High Street.
They were snogging in the yard.
They were snogging in the classroom.
They were snogging really hard.

They were snogging at the bus-stop
and in the canteen too.
They were snogging in the supermarket
standing in the queue.

They were snogging most of yesterday
and all the day before.
They were snogging in the changing room
just behind the door.

They were snogging on the playing field,
though it was lousy weather.
They snog so much, I think their lips
are superglued together.

Charles Thomson

Custard Pie

Poems that are jokes that are poems.
Chosen by Pie Corbett.

Love Poem

Her eyes were bright
as she reached out
and touched me with her
smooth, white hand.

I trembled,
excitedly;
as she happened
to be clutching
a live electric cable,
at the time.

Harry Munn